W9-BCI-647

784.4
EMM
Emmer, Rae
Band = Banda

$15.95
BC#32457105001345

DATE DUE	BORROWER'S NAME

784.4   BC#32457105001345 $15.95
EMM   Emmer, Rae
             Band = Banda

Morrill ES
Chicago Public Schools
6011 S Rockwell St.
Chicago, IL 60629

Bilingual Edition

READING POWER

Edición Bilingüe

School Activities

Band

Banda

Rae Emmer

The Rosen Publishing Group's
PowerKids Press™ & **Buenas Letras**™
New York

1

Published in 2003 by The Rosen Publishing Group, Inc.
29 East 21st Street, New York, NY 10010
Copyright © 2003 by The Rosen Publishing Group, Inc.

First Bilingual Edition 2003
First Edition in English 2002

Book Design: Christopher Logan, Victoria Johnson
Photo Credits: Cover, pp. 4, 6–21 by Maura Boruchow; p. 5 © Tony Freeman/PhotoEdit

Thanks to Beverly Hills Middle School

Emmer, Rae
Band/Banda/Rae Emmer ; traducción al español: Spanish Educational Publishing
p. cm. — (School Activities)
Includes bibliographical references and index.
ISBN 0-8239-6902-9 (lib. bdg.)
1. Bands (Music)—Juvenile literature. [1. Bands (Music) 2. Spanish Language Materials—Bilingual.] I. Title. II.School activities (New York, N.Y.)

Printed in The United States of America

Contents _____

Marching Bands	4
School Band	8
Practicing	14
The Concert	18
Glossary	22
Resources	23
Index	24

_____ Contenido

Las bandas de músicos	4
La banda de la escuela	8
Práctica	14
El concierto	18
Glosario	22
Recursos	23
Índice	24

I like marching bands.

_____

Me gustan las bandas.

I like the tuba best.

La tuba es el instrumento
que más me gusta.

We have a band at our school.

En nuestra escuela
tenemos una banda.

I play the tuba in the school band.

Yo toco la tuba en la banda.

The tuba is very big. It is the biggest brass horn in the band.

La tuba es muy grande.
Es el instrumento de viento más grande de la banda.

I play my tuba at home.
I practice every night.
Practice helps me to play better.

Toco la tuba en mi casa.
Practico todas las noches.
Cuanto más practico,
mejor toco.

We also practice at school. Our teacher helps us play together.

También practicamos
en la escuela.
El maestro nos enseña
a tocar juntos.

We have a concert after we have practiced. We play for our families.

Después de practicar, damos un concierto para nuestras familias.

One day I will play in the marching band.

Cuando sea grande,
voy a tocar en una banda.

Glossary

brass horn (**bras horn**) a musical object that is made of metal

concert (**kahn**-suhrt) a musical performance

marching band (**march**-ihng **band**) a group of people who walk in step while playing music

practice (**prak**-tihs) to do something again and again to learn to do it well

tuba (**too**-buh) a large brass horn that has a deep tone

Glosario

banda (la) grupo de músicos que marchan mientras que tocan música

concierto (el) actuación musical

instrumento de viento (el) instrumento musical por el que se sopla

practicar hacer algo una y otra vez para aprender a hacerlo bien

tuba (la) instrumento de viento grande que tiene un sonido muy bajo

Resources / Recursos

Here are more books to read about the bands:
Otros libros que puedes leer sobre bandas:

Musical Instruments from A–Z
by Bobbie Kalman
Crabtree Publishing (1997)

Young Person's Guide to Music
by Neil Ardley
DK Publishing (1995)

Web sites
Due to the changing nature of Internet links, PowerKids Press has developed an online list of Web sites related to the subject of this book. This site is updated regularly. Please use this link to access the list:

Sitios web
Debido a las constantes modificaciones en los sitios de Internet, PowerKids Press ha desarrollado una guía on-line de sitios relacionados al tema de este libro. Nuestro sitio web se actualiza constantemente. Por favor utiliza la siguiente dirección para consultar la lista:

http://www.buenasletraslinks.com/chl/tmb

Word count in English: 87
Número de palabras en español: 86

Index

B
brass, 12

C
concert, 18

H
horn, 12

M
marching band, 4, 20

S
school band, 10

T
tuba, 6, 10, 12, 14

Índice

B
banda, 4, 10, 20

C
concierto, 18

I
instrumento de viento, 12

P
practicar, 14, 17

T
tuba, 7, 10, 12, 14